Bread Machine Cookbook

Bread Machine Recipes for Baking Perfect Homemade Bread with Different Flavors and Ingredients

Linda Gilmore

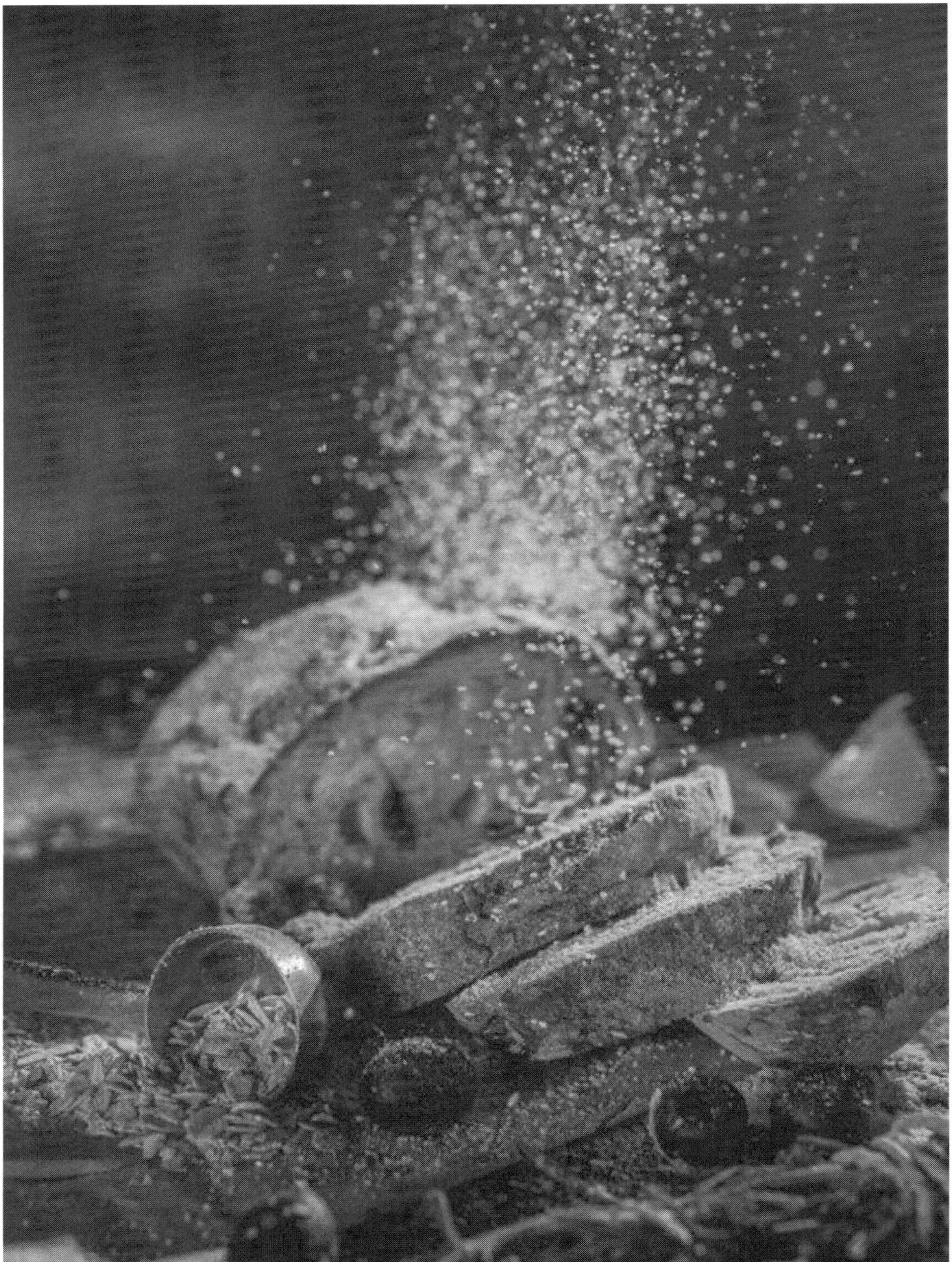

Table of Contents

Introduction 5

Everyday Bread 8

   Corn Bread 8

   Classic White Bread 10

   Coconut Bran Bread 12

   Milk White Bread 14

   Sour Cream Wheat Bread 16

   Vanilla Milk Bread 18

   Corn Bread 20

   Cream Hazelnut Bread 22

   Poppy Seeds Bread 24

   Coffee Rye Bread 26

Spice Bread 28

   Cheese Bread 28

   Green Cheese Bread 30

   Herb Bread 32

   Olive Bread 34

   Cumin Bread 36

   Raisin Bread 38

   Mozzarella Whole-Grain Bread 40

   Rosemary Bread 42

   Mozzarella Bread 44

   Fragrant Cinnamon Bread 46

Meat Bread 48

   French Ham Bread 48

   Chicken Bread 50

   Onion Bacon Bread 52

   Vegetable Bread 54

   Cheddar Sausage Bread 56

Vegetable Bread 58

3

Curd Bread..*58*

Crispy Bread with Fried Onion *60*

Savory Tomato Cheese Bread...........................*62*

Saffron Tomato Bread *64*

Carrot Oat Bread *66*

Zucchini Bread..*68*

Cumin Tomato Bread.......................................*70*

Savory Horseradish Bread *72*

Vegetable Bread..*74*

Celery Bread *76*

Sweet Bread **78**

Citrus Bread..*78*

Raisin Cake *80*

Apple Bread..*82*

Lemon Cake *84*

Soft Coconut Bread...*86*

Pineapple Coconut Bread *88*

Citrus Bread..*90*

Orange Bread *92*

Strawberry Bread *94*

Peach Bread *96*

Useful Tools **98**

From the Author...*99*

Our Recommendations..................................*100*

Recipe Index...**102**

Introduction

I used to believe that baking bread was incredibly difficult. Perhaps so difficult that only people with very special skills and equipment could do it well. Do you believe that, too?

If so, don't! **Anyone can bake bread if their kitchen** is big enough to accommodate a bread machine. As for advice and tips — everything a novice baker would need is in this book.

Why would someone make homemade bread in the first place? Everyone has their own answer to this question, but there are still some very common reasons. We are used to buying bread in a shop, and just as used to muttering about it unhappily. Some say that it stales too quickly, and others grumble that it tastes nothing as it used to... Only the name is the same. Is that true, or are we just nostalgic for another time?

Actually, the bread really has changed. Most modern loaves and baguettes contain some

5

"improving agents" — preservatives, emulsifiers, and other unappetizing things. Here you have the main answer to our "Why?" **Homemade bread contains only what you've put in it**: flour, water, and yeast, complemented by any other natural products of your choice.

At home, you can bake exactly the bread that you like. Add some seeds, dried fruit, or whatever else you want to make the combination precisely to your taste! How much will such a unique loaf of bread cost? No more than the cost of the ingredients plus about ten minutes of your time to load them into the bread machine. It's definitely cheaper than in a shop. **The low cost of homemade bread combined with its high quality** is another argument in favor of a bread machine.

These days, it seems we are always in a hurry and constantly short of time — the pace of modern life is so terribly fast that it has split our life into short segments of "I can make it" and "I cannot make it." And the faster we have to run, the more we miss out on feeling warm, fuzzy, and cozy — feeling at home...

As a culinary art, **bread making allows a lot of room for creativity**. It's a completely new world, and a big one. You can bake a new loaf every day for a year and make no two loaves exactly the same. On the other hand, you can select five favorite recipes and bring them to perfection. The only thing I have to warn you about — **this hobby is rather addictive**. It's really incredible watching water and flour turn into the miracle of homemade bread. And even more incredible is knowing that the creator of this miracle is no one but you. Bread machines are just modest (but very crafty!) assistants who can do all the routine work.

Of course, to cook a tasty bread, the **home baker has to learn at least the most basic things.** Well, that's obvious: even cooking pasta requires some theory. Those who have tried putting raw pasta into cold water know what I mean.

The first section of my book is devoted to casual breads. If your new bread machine is unpacked and ready, flour and yeast are bought, and you can't wait to start, this is the chapter to turn to immediately. In just about four hours, you will be the happy owner of your first self-baked bread!

If you are a bit — or even much more — experienced in bread making, you can skip this section. In the following sections, you will find **recipes for bread made with vegetables, spices, and cheese.** The last section is a treat for those who like **sweet baking**. With any of these recipes, you can make bread in either a bread machine or an oven.

We'll start with the simplest of the recipes and then... then everything will depend on you and you alone. If something seems too difficult or confusing, just remind yourself that other bread makers have managed and there is no reason why you cannot. If something seems too simple, perhaps you need to move on to the next section and master new recipes.

I wish you a tasty bread!

Everyday Bread

CORN BREAD

A fresh loaf with a light yellow, tender crumb and a sunny crust is a great way to cheer yourself up on a rainy day. Add a dusting of fine-ground flour to your gingerbread men, and they will obediently keep the right shape and won't stick to your hands. Bread makes a great pairing with light vegetable soups and stews, and if you dip a slice into some milk whisked with eggs and then crisp it in a frying pan, you will get some delicious croutons.

Total time: 2½ hours | Yield: 1 loaf (2½ pounds) / 8 servings
Program: Basic/White bread/Fast | Crust: Medium

INGREDIENTS

1¼ cups (300 ml) lukewarm whole milk

2-3 Tbsp. corn oil

3 cups (550 g) all-purpose wheat flour/white/ bread, sifted

¾ cup (150 g) cornflour

4 whole eggs

1 Tbsp. (10 g) baking powder

2 Tbsp. (50 g) white sugar

1 tsp. kosher salt

STEPS TO MAKE IT

1. Place all the dry and liquid ingredients in the pan and follow the instructions for your bread machine.
2. Pay particular attention to measuring the ingredients. Use a measuring cup, measuring spoon, and kitchen scales to do so.
3. Set the baking program to BASIC and the crust type to MEDIUM.
4. If the dough is too dense or too wet, adjust the amount of flour and liquid in the recipe.
5. When the program has ended, take the pan out of the bread machine and let cool for 5 minutes.
6. Shake the loaf out of the pan. If necessary, use a spatula.
7. Wrap the bread with a kitchen towel and set it aside for an hour. Otherwise, you can cool it on a wire rack.

NUTRITION GUIDELINES (PER SERVING)

Calories 304; Total Fat 7.3g; Saturated Fat 2g; Cholesterol 85g; Sodium 343mg; Total Carbohydrate 50.1g; Dietary Fiber 2.1g; Total Sugars 5.1g; Protein 9.6g

CLASSIC WHITE BREAD

Bread. Plain bread. It doesn't really need any add-ons. It's so good that even butter or jam seems needless. And the crispy crust is more than delicious.

Total time: 3½ hours | Yield: 1 loaf (1½ pounds) / 8 servings
Program: Basic/White bread | Crust: Medium

INGREDIENTS

½ cup (110 ml) lukewarm whole milk

1 cup (210 ml) lukewarm water

2 Tbsp. white sugar

1 Tbsp. butter, melted

1 tsp. salt

3½ cups (450 g) wheat bread machine /white/all-purpose flour

2 Tbsp. bread machine yeast

STEPS TO MAKE IT

1. Place all the dry and liquid ingredients in the pan and follow the instructions for your bread machine.
2. Pay particular attention to measuring the ingredients. Use a measuring cup, measuring spoon, and kitchen scales to do so.
3. Set the baking program to BASIC and the crust type to MEDIUM.
4. If the dough is too dense or too wet, adjust the amount of flour and liquid in the recipe.
5. When the program has ended, take the pan out of the bread machine and let cool for 5 minutes.
6. Shake the loaf out of the pan. If necessary, use a spatula.
7. Wrap the bread with a kitchen towel and set it aside for an hour. Otherwise, you can cool it on a wire rack.

NUTRITION GUIDELINES (PER SERVING)

Calories 240; Total Fat 2.4g; Saturated Fat 1.2g; Cholesterol 5g; Sodium 312mg; Total Carbohydrate 46.6g; Dietary Fiber 2.1g; Total Sugars 3.8g; Protein 7.3g

COCONUT BRAN BREAD

Adding milk or cream to the dough gives a crispy brown crust, but the crumb often gets a bit stodgy. You can add some bran or wholemeal flour to make the bread bolder and lighter.

Total time: 3½ hours | Yield: 1 loaf (2½ pounds) / 8 servings
Program: Basic / White bread | Crust: Light / Medium

INGREDIENTS

3¾ cups (480 g) wheat bread machine / white flour

1¾ cups (200 g) bran meal

1¼ cups (300 ml) cream

1/3 cup (70 ml) coconut milk

2 Tbsp. liquid honey

2 Tbsp. vegetable oil

2 tsp. bread machine yeast

2 tsp. salt

STEPS TO MAKE IT

1. Place all the dry and liquid ingredients in the pan and follow the instructions for your bread machine.
2. Pay particular attention to measuring the ingredients. Use a measuring cup, measuring spoon, and kitchen scales to do so.
3. Set the baking program to BASIC and the crust type to MEDIUM.
4. If the dough is too dense or too wet, adjust the amount of flour and liquid in the recipe.
5. When the program has ended, take the pan out of the bread machine and let cool for 5 minutes.
6. Shake the loaf out of the pan. If necessary, use a spatula.
7. Wrap the bread with a kitchen towel and set it aside for an hour. Otherwise, you can cool it on a wire rack.

NUTRITION GUIDELINES (PER SERVING)

Calories 348; Total Fat 8.6g; Saturated Fat 4.2g; Cholesterol 7g; Sodium 641mg; Total Carbohydrate 59.4g; Dietary Fiber 3.2g; Total Sugars 6.7g; Protein 8.1g

MILK WHITE BREAD

Add some butter and sugar to get a neat, light-brown crust. Soften the butter at room temperature and mix it into the milk before filling the pan. For a glossy top, carefully open the bread machine and gently brush the bread with some egg yolks whisked in milk about 5 to 8 minutes before the end of the baking process.

Total time: 3½ hours | Yield: 1 loaf (2½ pounds) / 8 servings
Program: Basic / White bread | Crust: Light / Medium

INGREDIENTS

1¼ cups (280 ml / 9½ oz) lukewarm whole milk

5¼ cups (680 g) bread machine wheat flour

2 Tbsp. butter, softened

2 tsp. bread machine yeast

1 Tbsp. white sugar

2 tsp. salt

STEPS TO MAKE IT

1. Place all the dry and liquid ingredients in the pan and follow the instructions for your bread machine.
2. Pay particular attention to measuring the ingredients. Use a measuring cup, measuring spoon, and kitchen scales to do so.
3. Set the baking program to BASIC and the crust type to MEDIUM.
4. If the dough is too dense or too wet, adjust the amount of flour and liquid in the recipe.
5. When the program has ended, take the pan out of the bread machine and let cool for 5 minutes.
6. Shake the loaf out of the pan. If necessary, use a spatula.
7. Wrap the bread with a kitchen towel and set it aside for an hour. Otherwise, you can cool it on a wire rack.

NUTRITION GUIDELINES (PER SERVING)

Calories 352; Total Fat 4.5g; Saturated Fat 2.4g; Cholesterol 11g; Sodium 622mg; Total Carbohydrate 66.4g; Dietary Fiber 2.4g; Total Sugars 3.4g; Protein 10.1g

SOUR CREAM WHEAT BREAD

Your bread machine can bake some really awesome, crusty, yeast-leavened wheat bread. It's good for everyday use. It goes well with both jam and bacon. When choosing the vegetable oil for the recipe keep in mind that its flavor will come through in the bread.

Total time: 3½ hours | Yield: 1 loaf (2½ pounds) / 8 servings
Program: Basic / White bread | Crust: Light / Medium

INGREDIENTS

1¼ cups (280 ml / 9½ oz) lukewarm whole milk

5¼ cups (680 g) wheat bread machine flour

2 Tbsp. vegetable oil

2 Tbsp. sour cream

2 tsp. bread machine yeast

1 Tbsp. white sugar

2 tsp. kosher salt

STEPS TO MAKE IT

1. Place all the dry and liquid ingredients in the pan and follow the instructions for your bread machine.
2. Pay particular attention to measuring the ingredients. Use a measuring cup, measuring spoon, and kitchen scales to do so.
3. Set the baking program to BASIC and the crust type to MEDIUM.
4. If the dough is too dense or too wet, adjust the amount of flour and liquid in the recipe.
5. After the final mixing of the dough, smear the surface of the product with sour cream.
6. When the program has ended, take the pan out of the bread machine and let cool for 5 minutes.
7. Shake the loaf out of the pan. If necessary, use a spatula.
8. Wrap the bread with a kitchen towel and set it aside for an hour. Otherwise, you can cool it on a wire rack.
9. Cool, serve and enjoy.

NUTRITION GUIDELINES (PER SERVING)

Calories 344; Total Fat 4.9g; Saturated Fat 1.2g; Cholesterol 1g; Sodium 585mg; Total Carbohydrate 64.6g; Dietary Fiber 2.4g; Total Sugars 1.7g; Protein 8.9g

VANILLA MILK BREAD

My kids prefer milk bread over any other. It always comes out with a nicely crisped crust and very tender crumbs. You can adjust the milk and water proportion to your taste or use some cream powder.

Total time: 3½ hours | Yield: 1 loaf (2½ pounds) / 8 servings
Program: Basic / White bread | Crust: Light / Medium

INGREDIENTS

4½ cups (580 g) wheat bread machine flour

1¾ cups (370 ml / 12½ oz) lukewarm whole milk

1 Tbsp. white sugar

1 packet vanilla sugar

2 Tbsp. extra-virgin olive oil

2 tsp. bread machine yeast

2 tsp. sea salt

STEPS TO MAKE IT

1. Place all the dry and liquid ingredients in the pan and follow the instructions for your bread machine.
2. Pay particular attention to measuring the ingredients. Use a measuring cup, measuring spoon, and kitchen scales to do so.
3. Set the baking program to BASIC and the crust type to MEDIUM.
4. If the dough is too dense or too wet, adjust the amount of flour and liquid in the recipe.
5. When the program has ended, take the pan out of the bread machine and let cool for 5 minutes.
6. Shake the loaf out of the pan. If necessary, use a spatula.
7. Wrap the bread with a kitchen towel and set it aside for an hour. Otherwise, you can cool it on a wire rack.

NUTRITION GUIDELINES (PER SERVING)

Calories 328; Total Fat 5.7g; Saturated Fat 1.4g; Cholesterol 4g; Sodium 610mg; Total Carbohydrate 59.1g; Dietary Fiber 2.1g; Total Sugars 4.6g; Protein 9.4g

CORN BREAD

Total time: 3½ hours | Yield: 1 loaf (2½ pounds) / 8 servings
Program: Basic / White bread | Crust: Light / Medium

INGREDIENTS

3½ cups (480 g) cornflour

1½ cups (200 g) bread machine wheat flour, sifted

2 Tbsp. butter, softened

½ cup cornflakes

1 Tbsp. white sugar

2 tsp. bread machine yeast

2 tsp. kosher salt

STEPS TO MAKE IT

1. Place all the dry and liquid ingredients in the pan and follow the instructions for your bread machine.
2. Pay particular attention to measuring the ingredients. Use a measuring cup, measuring spoon, and kitchen scales to do so.
3. Set the baking program to BASIC and the crust type to MEDIUM.
4. If the dough is too dense or too wet, adjust the amount of flour and liquid in the recipe.
5. After the final mixing of the dough, moisten the surface of the product with water and sprinkle with cornflakes.
6. When the program has ended, take the pan out of the bread machine and let cool for 5 minutes.
7. Shake the loaf out of the pan. If necessary, use a spatula.
8. Wrap the bread with a kitchen towel and set it aside for an hour. Otherwise, you can cool it on a wire rack.

NUTRITION GUIDELINES (PER SERVING)

Calories 319; Total Fat 5.1g; Saturated Fat 2.1g; Cholesterol 8g; Sodium 634mg; Total Carbohydrate 62.3g; Dietary Fiber 4.8g; Total Sugars 2.1g; Protein 7.3g

CREAM HAZELNUT BREAD

Bread made with cornmeal can boast a nice color and ideal density, but the taste of cornbread is rather neutral. Therefore, it often asks for an intensifier. A great option here is adding some hazelnuts to the crust. Cornbread matches perfectly with bacon and scrambled eggs.

Total time: 2½ hours | Yield: 1 loaf (2½ pounds) / 8 servings
Program: Fast | Crust: Medium

INGREDIENTS

3½ cups (450 g) wheat bread machine flour

1¾ cups (230 g) cornflour

5 ounces (150 ml) cream

2 Tbsp. vegetable oil

2 tsp. bread machine yeast

1 Tbsp. sugar

½ cup hazelnuts, ground

2 tsp. sea salt

STEPS TO MAKE IT

1. Place all the dry and liquid ingredients in the pan and follow the instructions for your bread machine.
2. Pay particular attention to measuring the ingredients. Use a measuring cup, measuring spoon, and kitchen scales to do so.
3. Set the baking program to FAST and the crust type to MEDIUM.
4. If the dough is too dense or too wet, adjust the amount of flour and liquid in the recipe.
5. After the dough finishes mixing, moisten the surface of the product with water and sprinkle with hazelnut.
6. When the program has ended, take the pan out of the bread machine and let cool for 5 minutes.
7. Shake the loaf out of the pan. If necessary, use a spatula.
8. Wrap the bread with a kitchen towel and set it aside for an hour. Otherwise, you can cool it on a wire rack.
9. Enjoy!

NUTRITION GUIDELINES (PER SERVING)

Calories 405; Total Fat 11.8g; Saturated Fat 3.6g; Cholesterol 13g; Sodium 607mg; Total Carbohydrate 66.3g; Dietary Fiber 4g; Total Sugars 3.4g; Protein 9.1g

POPPY SEEDS BREAD

Total time: 3½ hours | Yield: 1 loaf (2½ pounds) / 8 servings
Program: Basic / White Bread | Crust: Medium

INGREDIENTS

3½ cups bread machine wheat flour

1¾ cups (230 g) cornflour

5 ounces sour cream

2 Tbsp. corn oil

2 tsp. bread machine yeast

1 Tbsp. sugar

2 tsp. salt

poppy seeds (for sprinkling)

STEPS TO MAKE IT

1. Place all the dry and liquid ingredients in the pan and follow the instructions for your bread machine.
2. Pay particular attention to measuring the ingredients. Use a measuring cup, measuring spoon, and kitchen scales to do so.
3. Set the baking program to BASIC and the crust type to MEDIUM.
4. If the dough is too dense or too wet, adjust the amount of flour and liquid in the recipe.
5. After finishing mixing the dough, moisten the surface of the product with water and sprinkle with poppy seeds.
6. When the program has ended, take the pan out of the bread machine and let cool for 5 minutes.
7. Shake the loaf out of the pan. If necessary, use a spatula.
8. Wrap the bread with a kitchen towel and set it aside for an hour. Otherwise, you can cool it on a wire rack.
9. Your bread is now ready to serve.

NUTRITION GUIDELINES (PER SERVING)

Calories 374; Total Fat 9.2g; Saturated Fat 3g; Cholesterol 8g; Sodium 594mg; Total Carbohydrate 64.3g; Dietary Fiber 3.7g; Total Sugars 2g; Protein 8.6g

COFFEE RYE BREAD

This bread contains the classic combination of wheat and rye flours. Rye flour gives the bread some sourness and a rich rye flavor. However, you have to watch the loaf in the pan very carefully. Make sure there is no uncooked dough at the bottom.

Total time: 2 - 3 hours | Yield: 1 loaf (1 pounds) / 6 servings
Program: Basic / White Bread | Crust: Light

INGREDIENTS:

- ½ cup lukewarm water
- ¼ cup brewed coffee (80 degrees F)
- 2 Tbsp. dark molasses
- 5 tsp. brown sugar
- 4 tsp. unsalted butter, softened
- 1 Tbsp. powdered skim milk
- 1 tsp. kosher salt
- 4 tsp. unsweetened cocoa powder
- ⅔ cup dark rye flour
- ½ cup whole-wheat bread machine flour
- 1 tsp. caraway seeds
- 1 cup white bread machine flour
- 1½ tsp. bread machine yeast

STEPS TO MAKE IT:

1. Place all the dry and liquid ingredients in the pan and follow the instructions for your bread machine.
2. Pay particular attention to measuring the ingredients. Use a measuring cup, measuring spoon, and kitchen scales to do so.
3. Set the baking program to BASIC and the crust type to LIGHT.
4. If the dough is too dense or too wet, adjust the amount of flour and liquid in the recipe.
5. When the program has ended, take the pan out of the bread machine and let cool for 5 minutes.
6. Shake the loaf out of the pan. If necessary, use a spatula.
7. Wrap the bread with a kitchen towel and set it aside for an hour. Otherwise, you can cool it on a wire rack.

NUTRITION GUIDELINES (PER SERVING)

Calories 222; Total Fat 3.2g; Saturated Fat 1.8g; Cholesterol 7g; Sodium 415mg; Total Carbohydrate 42.9g; Dietary Fiber 4.7g; Total Sugars 6.8g; Protein 6.3g; Vitamin D 10mcg; Calcium 40mg; Iron 3mg; Potassium 297mg

Spice Bread

CHEESE BREAD

Cheese bread is always very tender and fragrant. Of course, the flavor depends on the kind of cheese you choose. If you want small chunks of cheese inside the bread, you'll have to take the dough out of the bread machine and manually mix the cheese in.

Total time: 3 hours | Yield: 1 loaf (2 pounds) / 8 servings
Program: Basic / White Bread | Crust: Light

INGREDIENTS

2½ cups wheat bread machine flour

1½ tsp. fresh bread machine yeast

½ cup lukewarm whole milk

1 Tbsp. butter, melted

2 Tbsp. sugar

½ tsp. kosher salt

2 whole eggs

2 tsp. fresh/dried rosemary, ground

3 Tbsp. parmesan (divided - 2 Tbsp. for dough and 1 Tbsp. for sprinkling)

2 cloves garlic, crushed

poppy seeds/sesame seeds, for sprinkling

STEPS TO MAKE IT

1. Place all the dry and liquid ingredients, except additives, in the pan and follow the instructions for your bread machine.
2. Pay particular attention to measuring the ingredients. Use a measuring cup, measuring spoon, and kitchen scales to do so.
3. Dissolve yeast in warm milk in a saucepan and add in the last turn.
4. Add the additives (rosemary, parmesan, and garlic) after the beep.
5. Set the baking program to BASIC and the crust type to LIGHT.
6. If the dough is too dense or too wet, adjust the amount of flour and liquid in the recipe.
7. Make incisions and smear the top with milk; sprinkle with poppy/sesame seeds and/or parmesan.
8. When the program has ended, take the pan out of the bread machine and let cool for 5 minutes.
9. Shake the loaf out of the pan. If necessary, use a spatula. Wrap the bread with a kitchen towel and set it aside for an hour. Otherwise, you can cool it on a wire rack.

NUTRITION GUIDELINES (PER SERVING)

Calories 212; Total Fat 4.6g; Saturated Fat 2.1g; Cholesterol 49g; Sodium 214mg; Total Carbohydrate 34.8g; Dietary Fiber 1.5g; Total Sugars 3.9g; Protein 7.6g

GREEN CHEESE BREAD

Whole-grain bread is known for its very distinct almost nutty aroma, but the flour itself behaves very differently from ordinary fine flour. Therefore, you'll have to carefully watch the loaf and adjust the amount of dry and liquid ingredients. The chances for a neat dome-shaped top aren't high. This bread is likely to sag a little. Such bread also stales faster, so try to eat it in the first days after baking.

Total time: 3 hours | Yield: 1 loaf (1½ pounds) / 8 servings
Program: Basic / White Bread | Crust: Dark

INGREDIENTS

¾ cup lukewarm water

1 Tbsp. sugar

1 tsp. kosher salt

2 Tbsp. green cheese

1 cup wheat bread machine flour

9/10 cup whole-grain flour, finely ground

1 tsp. bread machine yeast

1 tsp. ground paprika

STEPS TO MAKE IT

1. Place all the dry and liquid ingredients, except paprika, in the pan and follow the instructions for your bread machine.
2. Pay particular attention to measuring the ingredients. Use a measuring cup, measuring spoon, and kitchen scales to do so.
3. Dissolve yeast in warm milk in a saucepan and add in the last turn.
4. Add paprika after the beep or place it in the dispenser of the bread machine.
5. Set the baking program to BASIC and the crust type to DARK.
6. If the dough is too dense or too wet, adjust the amount of flour and liquid in the recipe.
7. When the program has ended, take the pan out of the bread machine and let cool for 5 minutes.
8. Shake the loaf out of the pan. If necessary, use a spatula.
9. Wrap the bread with a kitchen towel and set it aside for an hour. Otherwise, you can cool it on a wire rack.

NUTRITION GUIDELINES (PER SERVING)

Calories 118; Total Fat 1g; Saturated Fat 0.4g; Cholesterol 2g; Sodium 304mg; Total Carbohydrate 23.6g; Dietary Fiber 2.3g; Total Sugars 1.6g; Protein 4.1g

HERB BREAD

Carrot bread is an excellent substitute for pumpkin bread. You can replace dried carrots with grated fresh ones or use carrot juice. If you choose any of those, make sure to adjust the amount of flour in the recipe.

Total time: 3½ hours | Yield: 1 loaf (2 pounds) / 8 servings
Program: Basic / White Bread | Crust: Medium

INGREDIENTS

3½ cups wheat bread machine flour

1 cup lukewarm water

1 Tbsp. kosher salt

1 Tbsp. light brown sugar

2 Tbsp. ground paprika

1 Tbsp. dried herbs

2 Tbsp. dried vegetables: sweet pepper (green and red), carrots

1½ Tbsp. extra-virgin olive oil

2 tsp. bread machine yeast

STEPS TO MAKE IT

1. Place all the dry and liquid ingredients, except additives, in the pan and follow the instructions for your bread machine.
2. Pay particular attention to measuring the ingredients. Use a measuring cup, measuring spoon, and kitchen scales to do so.
3. Set the baking program to BASIC and the crust type to MEDIUM.
4. Add the additives (paprika, dried vegetables, and herbs) after the beep or place them in the dispenser of the bread machine.
5. If the dough is too dense or too wet, adjust the amount of flour and liquid in the recipe.
6. When the program has ended, take the pan out of the bread machine and let cool for 5 minutes.
7. Shake the loaf out of the pan. If necessary, use a spatula.
8. Wrap the bread with a kitchen towel and set it aside for an hour. Otherwise, you can cool it on a wire rack.

NUTRITION GUIDELINES (PER SERVING)

Calories 240; Total Fat 3.6g; Saturated Fat 0.5g; Cholesterol 0g; Sodium 294mg; Total Carbohydrate 45.5g; Dietary Fiber 3g; Total Sugars 2g; Protein 6.5g

OLIVE BREAD

Take some canned green or black pitted olives and slice them crosswise into three or four segments. Dry the rings well and dredge them with flour. You can also mix some grated or diced cheese into the ready-to-cook dough, but then be sure to reduce the amount of salt you add to the dough.

Total time: 3½ hours | Yield: 1 loaf (2½ pounds) / 10 servings
Program: French Bread | Crust: Medium

INGREDIENTS

1 cup lukewarm water

½ cup olive brine

1 ½ Tbsp. melted butter

3 Tbsp. sugar

2 tsp. kosher salt

5 1/3 cups bread machine flour

2 tsp. bread machine yeast

20 olives, sliced

1½ tsp. Italian herbs

STEPS TO MAKE IT

1. Place all the dry and liquid ingredients, except olives, in the pan and follow the instructions for your bread machine.
2. Pay particular attention to measuring the ingredients. Use a measuring cup, measuring spoon, and kitchen scales to do so.
3. Set the baking program to FRENCH BREAD and the crust type to MEDIUM.
4. Add the olives after the beep or place them in the dispenser of the bread machine.
5. If the dough is too dense or too wet, adjust the amount of flour and liquid in the recipe.
6. When the program has ended, take the pan out of the bread machine and let cool for 5 minutes.
7. Shake the loaf out of the pan. If necessary, use a spatula.
8. Wrap the bread with a kitchen towel and set it aside for an hour. Otherwise, you can cool it on a wire rack.

NUTRITION GUIDELINES (PER SERVING)

Calories 386; Total Fat 6.6g; Saturated Fat 2.1g; Cholesterol 6; Sodium 899mg; Total Carbohydrate 71.7g; Dietary Fiber 3.4g; Total Sugars 4.7g; Protein 9.6g

CUMIN BREAD

Total time: 3½ hours | Yield: 1 loaf (2 pounds) / 8 servings
Program: Basic | Crust: Medium

INGREDIENTS

5 1/3 cups bread machine flour, sifted

1½ tsp. kosher salt

1½ Tbsp. sugar

1 Tbsp. bread machine yeast

1¾ cups lukewarm water

2 Tbsp. black cumin

3 Tbsp. sunflower oil

STEPS TO MAKE IT

1. Place all the dry and liquid ingredients in the pan and follow the instructions for your bread machine.
2. Pay particular attention to measuring the ingredients. Use a measuring cup, measuring spoon, and kitchen scales to do so.
3. Set the baking program to BASIC and the crust type to MEDIUM.
4. If the dough is too dense or too wet, adjust the amount of flour and liquid in the recipe.
5. When the program has ended, take the pan out of the bread machine and let cool for 5 minutes.
6. Shake the loaf out of the pan. If necessary, use a spatula.
7. Wrap the bread with a kitchen towel and set it aside for an hour. Otherwise, you can cool it on a wire rack.

NUTRITION GUIDELINES (PER SERVING)

Calories 368; Total Fat 6.5g; Saturated Fat 0.7g; Cholesterol 0; Sodium 444mg; Total Carbohydrate 67.1g; Dietary Fiber 2.7g; Total Sugars 2.5g; Protein 9.5g

RAISIN BREAD

Smaller additives like poppy or sesame seeds are added to the dough immediately, and larger ones like raisins and nuts are added after the signal or placed in the dispenser. Otherwise, the gluten in the flour won't develop correctly.

Total time: 3½ hours　|　Yield: 1 loaf (2½ pounds) / 10 servings
Program: Basic　|　Crust: Medium

INGREDIENTS

1½ cups lukewarm whole milk

2 Tbsp. sugar

1½ tsp. kosher salt

¼ tsp. powdered saffron

¼ tsp. turmeric

2 Tbsp. butter, melted

1 Tbsp. vanilla sugar

4½ cups bread machine wheat flour

1 tsp. bread machine yeast

1 cup raisins

STEPS TO MAKE IT

1. Place all the dry and liquid ingredients, except raisins, in the pan and follow the instructions for your bread machine.
2. Pay particular attention to measuring the ingredients. Use a measuring cup, measuring spoon, and kitchen scales to do so.
3. Set the baking program to BASIC and the crust type to MEDIUM.
4. Add the raisins after the beep or place them in the dispenser of the bread machine.
5. If the dough is too dense or too wet, adjust the amount of flour and liquid in the recipe.
6. When the program has ended, take the pan out of the bread machine and let cool for 5 minutes.
7. Shake the loaf out of the pan. If necessary, use a spatula.
8. Wrap the bread with a kitchen towel and set it aside for an hour. Otherwise, you can cool it on a wire rack.

NUTRITION GUIDELINES (PER SERVING)

Calories 378; Total Fat 4.9g; Saturated Fat 2.6g; Cholesterol 11; Sodium 485mg; Total Carbohydrate 74.4g; Dietary Fiber 2.7g; Total Sugars 16.5g; Protein 9.6g

MOZZARELLA WHOLE-GRAIN BREAD

Total time: 3½ hours | Yield: 1 loaf (2 pounds) / 8 servings
Program: Basic | Crust: Dark

INGREDIENTS

1 cup mixture: milk + egg

½ cup Mozzarella cheese

2¼ cups bread machine flour

¾ cup whole-grain flour

2 Tbsp. sugar

1 tsp. sea salt

2 tsp. dried oregano

1½ tsp. bread machine yeast

STEPS TO MAKE IT

1. Place all the dry and liquid ingredients in the pan and follow the instructions for your bread machine.
2. Pay particular attention to measuring the ingredients. Use a measuring cup, measuring spoon, and kitchen scales to do so.
3. Set the baking program to BASIC and the crust type to DARK.
4. If the dough is too dense or too wet, adjust the amount of flour and liquid in the recipe.
5. When the program has ended, take the pan out of the bread machine and let cool for 5 minutes.
6. Shake the loaf out of the pan. If necessary, use a spatula.
7. Wrap the bread with a kitchen towel and set it aside for an hour. Otherwise, you can cool it on a wire rack.

NUTRITION GUIDELINES (PER SERVING)

Calories 209; Total Fat 2.1g; Saturated Fat 0.8g; Cholesterol 24; Sodium 325mg; Total Carbohydrate 40.1g; Dietary Fiber 2.6g; Total Sugars 4.6g; Protein 7.7g

ROSEMARY BREAD

Thanks to the eggs, this bread rises really well. However, it also stales well. It's a great option for toasting. And a hint of rosemary will remind you that this recipe originated in Italy.

Total time: 3½ hours | Yield: 1 loaf (2 pounds) / 8 servings
Program: Basic | Crust: Medium

INGREDIENTS

2 whole eggs

¾ cup lukewarm water

1 tsp. bread machine yeast

3 cups white bread machine flour

1 tsp. sea salt

3 Tbsp. rosemary, freshly chopped

1 Tbsp. sugar

4 Tbsp. extra-virgin olive oil

1 cup raisins

small sprigs of rosemary for decoration

STEPS TO MAKE IT

1. Beat the eggs in a dish and then top with water.
2. Place all the dry and liquid ingredients, except raisins, in the pan and follow the instructions for your bread machine.
3. Pay particular attention to measuring the ingredients. Use a measuring cup, measuring spoon, and kitchen scales to do so.
4. Set the baking program to BASIC and the crust type to MEDIUM.
5. Add the raisins after the beep or place them in the dispenser of the bread machine.
6. If the dough is too dense or too wet, adjust the amount of flour and liquid in the recipe.
7. Before baking spread the sprigs of rosemary on the surface.
8. When the program has ended, take the pan out of the bread machine and let cool for 5 minutes.
9. Shake the loaf out of the pan. If necessary, use a spatula.
10. Wrap the bread with a kitchen towel and set it aside for an hour. Otherwise, you can cool it on a wire rack.

NUTRITION GUIDELINES (PER SERVING)

Calories 312; Total Fat 8.8g; Saturated Fat 1.5g; Cholesterol 41; Sodium 311mg; Total Carbohydrate 52.7g; Dietary Fiber 2.6g; Total Sugars 12.4g; Protein 7g

MOZZARELLA BREAD

If you prefer a more savory bread, sprinkle it with paprika or cumin. Italian herbs are also a great match.

Total time: 3½ hours | Yield: 1 loaf (2 pounds) / 10 servings
Program: Basic / White Bread | Crust: Dark

INGREDIENTS:

- *1 cup (milk + egg) mixture*
- *½ cup mozzarella cheese*
- *2¼ cups bread machine wheat flour*
- *¾ cup whole-grain flour*
- *2 Tbsp. sugar*
- *1 tsp. kosher salt*
- *2 tsp. dried oregano*
- *1½ tsp. bread machine yeast*

STEPS TO MAKE IT:

1. Place all the dry and liquid ingredients in the pan and follow the instructions for your bread machine.
2. Pay particular attention to measuring the ingredients. Use a measuring cup, measuring spoon, and kitchen scales to do so.
3. Set the baking program to BASIC and the crust type to DARK.
4. If the dough is too dense or too wet, adjust the amount of flour and liquid in the recipe.
5. When the program has ended, take the pan out of the bread machine and let cool for 5 minutes.
6. Shake the loaf out of the pan. If necessary, use a spatula.
7. Wrap the bread with a kitchen towel and set it aside for an hour. Otherwise, you can cool it on a wire rack.

NUTRITION GUIDELINES (PER SERVING)

Calories 157; Total Fat 1.2g; Saturated Fat 0.6g; Cholesterol 3g; Sodium 254mg; Total Carbohydrate 30.4g; Dietary Fiber 2g; Total Sugars 3.6g; Protein 5.9g; Vitamin D 0mcg; Calcium 42mg; Iron 2mg; Potassium 91mg

FRAGRANT CINNAMON BREAD

Total time: 2 - 3 hours | Yield: 1 loaf (1 pound) / 8 servings
Program: Basic / White Bread | Crust: Medium

INGREDIENTS:

⅔ cup lukewarm whole milk

1 whole egg, beaten

3 Tbsp. melted butter, cooled

⅓ cup sugar

⅓ tsp. kosher salt

1 tsp. ground cinnamon

2 cups white bread machine flour

1⅓ tsp. bread machine yeast

STEPS TO MAKE IT:

1. Place all the dry and liquid ingredients in the pan and follow the instructions for your bread machine.
2. Pay particular attention to measuring the ingredients. Use a measuring cup, measuring spoon, and kitchen scales to do so.
3. Set the baking program to BASIC and the crust type to MEDIUM.
4. If the dough is too dense or too wet, adjust the amount of flour and liquid in the recipe.
5. When the program has ended, take the pan out of the bread machine and let cool for 5 minutes.
6. Shake the loaf out of the pan. If necessary, use a spatula.
7. Wrap the bread with a kitchen towel and set it aside for an hour. Otherwise, you can cool it on a wire rack.

NUTRITION GUIDELINES (PER SERVING)

Calories 213; Total Fat 5.9g; Saturated Fat 3.2g; Cholesterol 34g; Sodium 146mg; Total Carbohydrate 34.6g; Dietary Fiber 1.1g; Total Sugars 9.4g; Protein 5.7g; Vitamin D 5mcg; Calcium 37mg; Iron 2mg; Potassium 66mg

Meat Bread

FRENCH HAM BREAD

Total time: 3½ hours | Yield: 1 loaf (2 pounds) / 10 servings
Program: French Bread | Crust: Medium

INGREDIENTS

3 1/3 cups wheat bread machine flour

1 cup ham, chopped

½ cup milk powder

1½ Tbsp. sugar

1 tsp. fresh yeast

1 tsp. kosher salt

2 Tbsp. parmesan cheese, grated

1 1/3 cups lukewarm water

2 Tbsp. extra-virgin olive oil

STEPS TO MAKE IT

1. Cut ham into cubes of ½ - 1 cm (approximately ¼ inch).
2. Place all the dry and liquid ingredients in the pan and follow the instructions for your bread machine.
3. Pay particular attention to measuring the ingredients. Use a measuring cup, measuring spoon, and kitchen scales to do so.
4. Set the baking program to FRENCH BREAD and the crust type to MEDIUM.
5. Add the additives after the beep or place them in the dispenser of the bread machine.
6. If the dough is too dense or too wet, adjust the amount of flour and liquid in the recipe.
7. When the program has ended, take the pan out of the bread machine and let cool for 5 minutes.
8. Shake the loaf out of the pan. If necessary, use a spatula.
9. Wrap the bread with a kitchen towel and set it aside for an hour. Otherwise, you can cool it on a wire rack.

NUTRITION GUIDELINES (PER SERVING)

Calories 287; Total Fat 5.5g; Saturated Fat 1.1g; Cholesterol 11g; Sodium 557mg; Total Carbohydrate 47.2g; Dietary Fiber 1.7g; Total Sugars 6.4g; Protein 11.4g

CHICKEN BREAD

Choosing the right butter is crucial for this bread. This secret ingredient can endow your bread with a unique flavor. I usually cook this bread with mustard butter. The hints of mustard make a great match with chicken. Those who are keen on mustard can also add 1 tsp. of dry mustard to the dough. However, it won't really impact the flavor unless you've added mustard oil.

Total time: 3½ hours | Yield: 1 loaf (2 pounds) / 10 servings
Program: Basic | Crust: Medium

INGREDIENTS

2 cups boiled chicken, chopped

1 cup lukewarm whole milk

3 cups wheat bread machine flour, sifted

1 Tbsp. bread machine yeast

1 whole egg

1 tsp. sugar

½ Tbsp. sea salt

2 Tbsp. extra-virgin olive oil

STEPS TO MAKE IT

1. Pre-cook the chicken. You can use a leg or fillet.
2. Separate the chicken from the bone and cut it into small pieces.
3. Place all the dry and liquid ingredients, except the chicken, in the pan and follow the instructions for your bread machine.
4. Pay particular attention to measuring the ingredients. Use a measuring cup, measuring spoon, and kitchen scales to do so.
5. Set the baking program to BASIC and the crust type to MEDIUM.
6. Add the chicken after the beep or place them in the dispenser of the bread machine.
7. If the dough is too dense or too wet, adjust the amount of flour and liquid in the recipe.
8. When the program has ended, take the pan out of the bread machine and let cool for 5 minutes.
9. Shake the loaf out of the pan. If necessary, use a spatula.
10. Wrap the bread with a kitchen towel and set it aside for an hour. Otherwise, you can cool it on a wire rack.

NUTRITION GUIDELINES (PER SERVING)

Calories 283; Total Fat 6.2g; Saturated Fat 1.4g; Cholesterol 50g; Sodium 484mg; Total Carbohydrate 38.4g; Dietary Fiber 1.6g; Total Sugars 2g; Protein 17.2g

ONION BACON BREAD

Always season your bread with your favorite spices (up to 1 tsp.) and herbs (up to 1 Tbsp.). This will make it unique and enrich the flavor and aroma.

Total time: 3 hours | Yield: 1 loaf (2½ pounds) / 12 servings
Program: Basic | Crust: Medium

INGREDIENTS

1½ cups lukewarm water

2 Tbsp. sugar

3 tsp. bread machine yeast

4½ cups bread machine flour

1 whole egg

2 tsp. sea salt

1 Tbsp. extra-virgin olive oil

3 small onions, chopped

1 cup fried bacon, chopped

STEPS TO MAKE IT

1. Place all the dry and liquid ingredients, except additives, in the pan and follow the instructions for your bread machine.
2. Pay particular attention to measuring the ingredients. Use a measuring cup, measuring spoon, and kitchen scales to do so.
3. Set the baking program to BASIC and the crust type to MEDIUM.
4. Add the additives after the beep or place them in the dispenser of the bread machine.
5. If the dough is too dense or too wet, adjust the amount of flour and liquid in the recipe.
6. When the program has ended, take the pan out of the bread machine and let cool for 5 minutes.
7. Shake the loaf out of the pan. If necessary, use a spatula.
8. Wrap the bread with a kitchen towel and set it aside for an hour. Otherwise, you can cool it on a wire rack.

NUTRITION GUIDELINES (PER SERVING)

Calories 391; Total Fat 9.7g; Saturated Fat 2.7g; Cholesterol 38g; Sodium 960mg; Total Carbohydrate 59.9g; Dietary Fiber 2.8g; Total Sugars 4.3g; Protein 14.7g

VEGETABLE BREAD

Bran will add a delicate nuttiness to the bread. Coarse-ground bran will make the bread "speckled." 1 to 2 Tbsp. of bran can be added to any kind of bread and will only make the bread better and healthier. There is considerably more bran in this recipe, however, so you will have to adjust the amount of water and flour to get a loaf of the desired consistency.

Total time: 3 hours | Yield: 1 loaf (2 pounds) / 10 servings
Program: Basic | Crust: Medium

INGREDIENTS

2½ cups wheat bread machine flour
½ cup bran
1 1/3 cups lukewarm water
1½ tsp. sea salt
1½ tsp. sugar
1½ Tbsp. mustard oil

1¼ tsp. bread machine yeast
2 tsp. powdered milk
1 cup bell pepper, chopped
¾ cup smoked fish, chopped
1 onion, chopped and fried

STEPS TO MAKE IT

1. Grind the onion and fry until golden brown.
2. Cut the fish into small pieces and the pepper into cubes.
3. Place all the dry and liquid ingredients, except additives, in the pan and follow the instructions for your bread machine.
4. Pay particular attention to measuring the ingredients. Use a measuring cup, measuring spoon, and kitchen scales to do so.
5. Set the baking program to BASIC and the crust type to MEDIUM.
6. Add the additives after the beep or place them in the dispenser of the bread machine.
7. If the dough is too dense or too wet, adjust the amount of flour and liquid in the recipe.
8. When the program has ended, take the pan out of the bread machine and let cool for 5 minutes.
9. Shake the loaf out of the pan. If necessary, use a spatula.
10. Wrap the bread with a kitchen towel and set it aside for an hour. Otherwise, you can cool it on a wire rack.
11. Bon Appetite!

NUTRITION GUIDELINES (PER SERVING)

Calories 208; Total Fat 3.8g; Saturated Fat 0.5g; Cholesterol 8g; Sodium 487mg; Total Carbohydrate 35.9g; Dietary Fiber 4.2g; Total Sugars 2.7g; Protein 7.2g

CHEDDAR SAUSAGE BREAD

Savory and filling, this bread makes a great stand-alone dish for a picnic. Its flavor depends on the cheese and sausages you choose for it. For more zest and flavor, you can add some onions or garlic, cumin, and dried paprika.

Total time: 4 hours | Yield: 1 loaf (2 pounds) / 10 servings
Program: Basic | Crust: Medium

INGREDIENTS

1 tsp. bread machine yeast

3½ cups wheat bread machine flour

1 tsp. kosher salt

1 Tbsp. sugar

1½ Tbsp. extra-virgin olive oil

2 Tbsp. smoked sausage

2 Tbsp. grated Cheddar cheese, grated

1 Tbsp. garlic, crushed

1 cup lukewarm water

STEPS TO MAKE IT

1. Cut the sausage into small cubes.
2. Place all the dry and liquid ingredients, except additives, in the pan and follow the instructions for your bread machine.
3. Pay particular attention to measuring the ingredients. Use a measuring cup, measuring spoon, and kitchen scales to do so.
4. Set the baking program to BASIC and the crust type to MEDIUM.
5. Add the additives after the beep or place them in the dispenser of the bread machine.
6. If the dough is too dense or too wet, adjust the amount of flour and liquid in the recipe.
7. When the program has ended, take the pan out of the bread machine and let cool for 5 minutes.
8. Shake the loaf out of the pan. If necessary, use a spatula.
9. Wrap the bread with a kitchen towel and set it aside for an hour. Otherwise, you can cool it on a wire rack.

NUTRITION GUIDELINES (PER SERVING)

Calories 260; Total Fat 5.6g; Saturated Fat 1.4g; Cholesterol 8g; Sodium 355mg; Total Carbohydrate 43.8g; Dietary Fiber 1.6g; Total Sugars 1.7g; Protein 7.7g

Vegetable Bread

CURD BREAD

You can replace dried onion with finely chopped fried onion. This bread is great with soups or vegetable stews.

Total time: 4 hours | Yield: 1 loaf (2½ pounds) / 12 servings
Program: Basic / White Bread | Crust: Medium

INGREDIENTS

¾ cup lukewarm water

3 2/3 cups wheat bread machine flour

¾ cup cottage cheese

2 Tbsp. softened butter

2 Tbsp. white sugar

1½ tsp. sea salt

1½ Tbsp. sesame seeds

2 Tbsp. dried onions

1¼ tsp. bread machine yeast

STEPS TO MAKE IT

1. Place all the dry and liquid ingredients in the pan and follow the instructions for your bread machine.
2. Pay particular attention to measuring the ingredients. Use a measuring cup, measuring spoon, and kitchen scales to do so.
3. Set the baking program to BASIC and the crust type to MEDIUM.
4. If the dough is too dense or too wet, adjust the amount of flour and liquid in the recipe.
5. When the program has ended, take the pan out of the bread machine and let cool for 5 minutes.
6. Shake the loaf out of the pan. If necessary, use a spatula.
7. Wrap the bread with a kitchen towel and set it aside for an hour. Otherwise, you can cool it on a wire rack.

NUTRITION GUIDELINES (PER SERVING)

Calories 277; Total Fat 4.7g; Saturated Fat 2.3g; Cholesterol 9g; Sodium 547mg; Total Carbohydrate 48.4g; Dietary Fiber 1.9g; Total Sugars 3.3g; Protein 9.4g

CRISPY BREAD WITH FRIED ONION

Total time: 4 hours | Yield: 1 loaf (1½ pounds) / 8 servings
Program: Basic / White Bread | Crust: Medium

INGREDIENTS

2½ cups bread machine flour
1 ½ tsp. kosher salt
1 Tbsp. sugar
1 tsp. bread machine yeast

1 cup lukewarm water
2 big onions, chopped and fried
3 Tbsp. extra-virgin olive oil

STEPS TO MAKE IT

1. Chop onions (do not grind) and fry in olive oil until golden brown. At the end of frying, lightly powder with flour so that they become even crispier.
2. Place all the dry and liquid ingredients, except the onion, in the pan and follow the instructions for your bread machine.
3. Pay particular attention to measuring the ingredients. Use a measuring cup, measuring spoon, and kitchen scales to do so.
4. Set the baking program to BASIC and the crust type to MEDIUM.
5. Add the onion after the beep.
6. If the dough is too dense or too wet, adjust the amount of flour and liquid in the recipe.
7. When the program has ended, take the pan out of the bread machine and let cool for 5 minutes.
8. Shake the loaf out of the pan. If necessary, use a spatula.
9. Wrap the bread with a kitchen towel and set it aside for an hour. Otherwise, you can cool it on a wire rack.

NUTRITION GUIDELINES (PER SERVING)

Calories 209; Total Fat 5.7g; Saturated Fat 0.8g; Cholesterol 0g; Sodium 441mg; Total Carbohydrate 35g; Dietary Fiber 2g; Total Sugars 3.2g; Protein 4.6g

SAVORY TOMATO CHEESE BREAD

This tomato bread is a perfect match for vegetables and fish. You can also add some seasoning (½ to 1 tsp.) or paprika. Tomato bread is great for toasting.

Total time: 3 hours | Yield: 1 loaf (1½ pounds) / 8 servings
Program: Basic / Italian Bread | Crust: Medium

INGREDIENTS

1 tsp. bread machine yeast

2 ½ cups wheat bread machine flour

1 ½ tsp. sea salt

1 Tbsp. sugar

1 Tbsp. extra-virgin olive oil

5 Tbsp. tomatoes, dried and filled with oil, chopped

½ cup Parmesan cheese, grated

1 cup lukewarm whole milk

STEPS TO MAKE IT

1. Place all the dry and liquid ingredients, except tomatoes, in the pan and follow the instructions for your bread machine.
2. Pay particular attention to measuring the ingredients. Use a measuring cup, measuring spoon, and kitchen scales to do so.
3. Set the baking program to BASIC and the crust type to MEDIUM.
4. Add the tomatoes after the beep or place them in the dispenser of the bread machine.
5. If the dough is too dense or too wet, adjust the amount of flour and liquid in the recipe.
6. When the program has ended, take the pan out of the bread machine and let cool for 5 minutes.
7. Shake the loaf out of the pan. If necessary, use a spatula.
8. Wrap the bread with a kitchen towel and set it aside for an hour. Otherwise, you can cool it on a wire rack.

NUTRITION GUIDELINES (PER SERVING)

Calories 209; Total Fat 5.1g; Saturated Fat 2.2g; Cholesterol 10g; Sodium 498mg; Total Carbohydrate 33.4g; Dietary Fiber 1.2g; Total Sugars 3.2g; Protein 7g

SAFFRON TOMATO BREAD

Gorgeous orange-colored bread with tomato flavor and tomato slices. This bread pairs beautifully with olives, cheese, and dry wine. You can add some ready-to-use Italian seasoning mix or create your own unique combination with thyme, basil, oregano, rosemary, dried garlic, and onion powder. Spice lovers can add up to 2 Tbsp. of herbal seasoning.

Total time: 3½ hours | Yield: 1 loaf (2 pounds) / 10 servings
Program: Basic / Italian Bread | Crust: Medium

INGREDIENTS

1 tsp. bread machine yeast

2½ cups wheat bread machine flour

1 Tbsp. panifarin

1½ tsp. kosher salt

1½ Tbsp. white sugar

2 Tbsp. extra-virgin olive oil

2 Tbsp. tomatoes, dried and chopped

1 Tbsp. tomato paste

½ cup firm cheese (cubes)

½ cup feta cheese

1 pinch saffron

1½ cups serum

STEPS TO MAKE IT

1. Five minutes before cooking, pour in dried tomatoes and 1 tablespoon of olive oil. Add the tomato paste and mix.
2. Place all the dry and liquid ingredients, except additives, in the pan and follow the instructions for your bread machine.
3. Pay particular attention to measuring the ingredients. Use a measuring cup, measuring spoon, and kitchen scales to do so.
4. Set the baking program to BASIC and the crust type to MEDIUM.
5. Add the additives after the beep or place them in the dispenser of the bread machine.
6. If the dough is too dense or too wet, adjust the amount of flour and liquid in the recipe.
7. When the program has ended, take the pan out of the bread machine and let cool for 5 minutes.
8. Shake the loaf out of the pan. If necessary, use a spatula.
9. Wrap the bread with a kitchen towel and set it aside for an hour. Otherwise, you can cool it on a wire rack.

NUTRITION GUIDELINES (PER SERVING)

Calories 260; Total Fat 9.2g; Saturated Fat 4g; Cholesterol 20g; Sodium 611mg; Total Carbohydrate 35.5g; Dietary Fiber 1.3g; Total Sugars 5.2g; Protein 8.9g

CARROT OAT BREAD

You will get a loaf with a light cream-colored fluffy crumb and a fragrant crust. Oatmeal catches and enhances other flavors, including the carrot, which will get even brighter in this recipe.

The dough will come out softer than a wheat one, and its air-whipped crumb may deform the top of the loaf, but this is not a problem. Before baking, brush the top of the bread with whisked egg whites, sprinkle it with oat-flakes, and brush with the whites again.

Total time: 1½ hours | Yield: 1 loaf (2½ pounds) / 12 servings
Program: Dough/Baking | Crust: Medium

INGREDIENTS

½ cup boiling water
2 carrots / 1 1/3 cup carrot juice)
1/3 cup oatmeal flour
4½ cups wheat bread machine flour
1/3 cup sesame seeds

3 Tbsp. sugar
3 Tbsp. butter, melted
3 Tbsp. oat bran
½ tsp. kosher salt
2 tsp. bread machine yeast

STEPS TO MAKE IT

1. Fry the bran in a dry frying pan and cool.
2. Brew oatmeal with boiling water and leave to cool down too.
3. Carrot juice is obtained by placing carrots in the juicer.
4. 2 tablespoons of carrot mill cake from the juicer add to the dough.
5. Place all the dry and liquid ingredients, except additives, in the pan and follow the instructions for your bread machine.
6. Pay particular attention to measuring the ingredients. Use a measuring cup, measuring spoon, and kitchen scales to do so.
7. Set the program to DOUGH.
8. Add the sesame seeds after the beep.
9. Then add the remaining additives.
10. If the dough is too dense or too wet, adjust the amount of flour and liquid in the recipe.
11. Bake on the BAKING program for 1 hour.
12. When the program has ended, take the pan out of the bread machine and let cool for 5 minutes.
13. Shake the loaf out of the pan. If necessary, use a spatula.
14. Wrap the bread with a kitchen towel and set it aside for an hour. Otherwise, you can cool it on a wire rack.

NUTRITION GUIDELINES (PER SERVING)

Calories 403; Total Fat 8.5g; Saturated Fat 3.4g; Cholesterol 11g; Sodium 243mg; Total Carbohydrate 71.4g; Dietary Fiber 4g; Total Sugars 6.7g; Protein 10.2g

ZUCCHINI BREAD

Zucchini bread is always fluffy and slightly moist, and you won't detect the typical zucchini smell or taste. You can replace the zucchini with cucumber, but then it's better to use a very ripe one. You can add fresh or dried herbs, to your taste. When kneading the dough, carefully watch its density, as the zucchini will release its moisture gradually as you work it.

Total time: 3½ hours | Yield: 1 loaf (2 pounds) / 10 servings
Program: Basic | Crust: Medium

INGREDIENTS

- 1 cup raw zucchini, grated
- 1 3/5 cups bread machine flour, sifted
- 1 ½ tsp. bread machine yeast
- ½ cup raw apple, grated
- 1 tsp. kosher salt
- ¼ tsp. ground cinnamon
- ¼ tsp. ground nutmeg
- 3 Tbsp. vegetable oil
- 2 Tbsp. butter, melted
- 1 whole egg
- 2 Tbsp. sugar

STEPS TO MAKE IT

1. Place all the dry and liquid ingredients, except zucchini and apples, in the pan and follow the instructions for your bread machine.
2. Pay particular attention to measuring the ingredients. Use a measuring cup, measuring spoon, and kitchen scales to do so.
3. Set the baking program to BASIC and the crust type to MEDIUM.
4. Add the apples and zucchini after the beep.
5. If the dough is too dense or too wet, adjust the amount of flour and liquid in the recipe.
6. When the program has ended, take the pan out of the bread machine and let cool for 5 minutes.
7. Shake the loaf out of the pan. If necessary, use a spatula.
8. Wrap the bread with a kitchen towel and set it aside for an hour. Otherwise, you can cool it on a wire rack.

NUTRITION GUIDELINES (PER SERVING)

Calories 193; Total Fat 8.9g; Saturated Fat 2.7g; Cholesterol 28g; Sodium 321mg; Total Carbohydrate 24.9g; Dietary Fiber 1.4g; Total Sugars 4.8g; Protein 3.8g

CUMIN TOMATO BREAD

Nothing tastes better than tomato bread. Dry-cured tomatoes should be as soft as raisins. Cut them into pieces, dredge with flour, and add to the dispenser. A tablespoon of Parmigiano-Reggiano is a perfect addition to the tomato bread.

Total time: 2 hours | Yield: 1 loaf (2½ pounds) / 12 servings
Program: Quick | Crust: Medium

INGREDIENTS

5¼ cups wheat bread machine flour

2 Tbsp. sun-dried tomatoes, chopped

2 cups lukewarm water

2 tsp. bread machine yeast

3 Tbsp. extra-virgin olive oil

1 Tbsp. cumin

2 Tbsp. sugar

2 tsp. sea salt

STEPS TO MAKE IT

1. Place all the dry and liquid ingredients in the pan and follow the instructions for your bread machine.
2. Pay particular attention to measuring the ingredients. Use a measuring cup, measuring spoon, and kitchen scales to do so.
3. Set the baking program to QUICK and the crust type to MEDIUM.
4. If the dough is too dense or too wet, adjust the amount of flour and liquid in the recipe.
5. When the program has ended, take the pan out of the bread machine and let cool for 5 minutes.
6. Shake the loaf out of the pan. If necessary, use a spatula.
7. Wrap the bread with a kitchen towel and set it aside for an hour. Otherwise, you can cool it on a wire rack.

NUTRITION GUIDELINES (PER SERVING)

Calories 361; Total Fat 6.1g; Saturated Fat 0.8g; Cholesterol 0g; Sodium 587mg; Total Carbohydrate 66.4g; Dietary Fiber 2.5g; Total Sugars 3.3g; Protein 9g

SAVORY HORSERADISH BREAD

Total time: 3½ hours | Yield: 1 loaf (2 pounds) / 10 servings
Program: Whole-Grain Bread | Crust: Medium

INGREDIENTS

3½ cups whole-grain flour

1½ cup lukewarm water

½ cup rye flour

2 Tbsp. horseradish, grated

2 Tbsp. parsley, chopped

1 Tbsp. dill seeds

1 Tbsp. sugar

1 Tbsp. butter, melted

1 tsp. bread machine yeast

1½ tsp. sea salt

STEPS TO MAKE IT

1. Place all the dry and liquid ingredients in the pan and follow the instructions for your bread machine.
2. Pay particular attention to measuring the ingredients. Use a measuring cup, measuring spoon, and kitchen scales to do so.
3. Set the baking program to WHOLE-GRAIN BREAD and the crust type to MEDIUM.
4. If the dough is too dense or too wet, adjust the amount of flour and liquid in the recipe.
5. When the program has ended, take the pan out of the bread machine and let cool for 5 minutes.
6. Shake the loaf out of the pan. If necessary, use a spatula.
7. Wrap the bread with a kitchen towel and set it aside for an hour. Otherwise, you can cool it on a wire rack.

NUTRITION GUIDELINES (PER SERVING)

Calories 248; Total Fat 2.3g; Saturated Fat 1g; Cholesterol 4g; Sodium 464mg; Total Carbohydrate 49.6g; Dietary Fiber 3.6g; Total Sugars 2g; Protein 7.1g

VEGETABLE BREAD

Total time: 2 - 3 hours | Yield: 1 loaf / 10 servings
Program: Basic / White Bread | Crust: Light

INGREDIENTS:

- ½ cup warm buttermilk
- 3 Tbsp. lukewarm water
- 1 Tbsp. canola oil
- 2/3 cup zucchini, shredded
- 2 Tbsp. green onions, chopped
- ¼ cup green bell pepper, chopped
- 2 Tbsp. Parmesan cheese, grated
- 2 Tbsp. white sugar
- 1 tsp. sea salt
- ½ tsp. lemon-pepper seasoning
- ½ cup old-fashioned oats
- 2½ cups bread machine flour
- 1½ tsp. bread machine yeast

STEPS TO MAKE IT:

1. Place all the dry and liquid ingredients in the pan and follow the instructions for your bread machine.
2. Pay particular attention to measuring the ingredients. Use a measuring cup, measuring spoon, and kitchen scales to do so.
3. Set the baking program to BASIC and the crust type to LIGHT.
4. If the dough is too dense or too wet, adjust the amount of flour and liquid in the recipe.
5. When the program has ended, take the pan out of the bread machine and let cool for 5 minutes.
6. Shake the loaf out of the pan. If necessary, use a spatula.
7. Wrap the bread with a kitchen towel and set it aside for an hour. Otherwise, you can cool it on a wire rack.

NUTRITION GUIDELINES (PER SERVING)

Calories 145; Total Fat 2.7g; Saturated Fat 0.7g; Cholesterol 2g; Sodium 228mg; Total Carbohydrate 25.6g; Dietary Fiber 1.3g; Total Sugars 3.4g; Protein 4.7g; Vitamin D 0mcg; Calcium 48mg; Iron 2mg; Potassium 98mg

CELERY BREAD

Total time: 3 hours 10 minutes | Yield: 1 loaf (1 pound) / 10 servings
Program: Basic / White Bread | Crust: Medium

INGREDIENTS:

- 1 can (10 ounces) cream of celery soup
- 3 Tbsp. low-fat milk, heated
- 1 Tbsp. vegetable oil
- 1¼ tsp. celery salt
- ¾ cup celery, fresh/sliced thin
- 1 Tbsp. celery leaves, fresh, chopped
- 1 whole egg
- ¼ tsp. white sugar
- 3 cups bread machine flour, sifted
- ¼ tsp. ginger, finely grated
- ½ cup quick-cooking oats
- 2 Tbsp. gluten
- 2 tsp. celery seeds
- 1 pack bread machine yeast

STEPS TO MAKE IT:

1. Place all the dry and liquid ingredients in the pan and follow the instructions for your bread machine.
2. Pay particular attention to measuring the ingredients. Use a measuring cup, measuring spoon, and kitchen scales to do so.
3. Set the baking program to BASIC and the crust type to MEDIUM.
4. If the dough is too dense or too wet, adjust the amount of flour and liquid in the recipe.
5. When the program has ended, take the pan out of the bread machine and let cool for 5 minutes.
6. Shake the loaf out of the pan. If necessary, use a spatula.
7. Wrap the bread with a kitchen towel and set it aside for an hour. Otherwise, you can cool it on a wire rack.

NUTRITION GUIDELINES (PER SERVING)

Calories 212; Total Fat 4g; Saturated Fat 0.9g; Cholesterol 20g; Sodium 249mg; Total Carbohydrate 35.2g; Dietary Fiber 1.9g; Total Sugars 1g; Protein 8.2g; Vitamin D 4mcg; Calcium 36mg; Iron 2mg; Potassium 138mg

Sweet Bread

CITRUS BREAD

This is a wonderful sweet bread with a classic combination of candied fruit and almonds. Its flavor and aroma get even brighter the second day. This bread can be served as a separate dish with tea, coffee, or milk.

Total time: 3 hours | Yield: 1 loaf / 10 servings
Program: Basic / White Bread / Sweet Bread | Crust: Light / Medium

INGREDIENTS:

1 whole egg

3 Tbsp. (40 g) butter, melted

1/3 cup (50 g, 1.5 oz) white sugar

1 Tbsp. vanilla sugar

½ cup tangerine juice

2/3 cup (150 ml, 8 oz) whole milk

1 tsp. kosher salt

4 cups (500 g, 18 oz) bread machine flour

1 Tbsp. bread machine yeast

¼ cup (50 g) candied oranges

¼ cup (50 g) candied lemon

2 tsp. lemon zest, finely grated

¼ cup (50 g) almonds, chopped

STEPS TO MAKE IT

1. Place all the dry and liquid ingredients, except candied fruits, zest, and almonds, in the pan and follow the instructions for your bread machine.
2. Pay particular attention to measuring the ingredients. Use a measuring cup, measuring spoon, and kitchen scales to do so.
3. Set the baking program to BASIC/SWEET BREAD and the crust type to MEDIUM.
4. Add candied fruits, zest, and chopped almonds after the beep.
5. If the dough is too dense or too wet, adjust the amount of flour and liquid in the recipe.
6. When the program has ended, take the pan out of the bread machine and let cool for 5 minutes.
7. Shake the loaf out of the pan. If necessary, use a spatula.
8. Wrap the bread with a kitchen towel and set it aside for an hour. Otherwise, you can cool it on a wire rack.

NUTRITION GUIDELINES (PER SERVING)

Calories 404

Total Fat 9.1 g, Saturated Fat 3.5 g, Cholesterol 34 mg, Sodium 345 mg, Total Carbohydrate 71.5 g, Dietary Fiber 2.9 g, Total Sugars 15.6 g, Protein 9.8 g, Vitamin D 5 mcg, Calcium 72 mg, Iron 4 mg, Potassium 195 mg

RAISIN CAKE

Raisins make a great addition to a dessert bread. Butter and sugar give it awesome crispiness. You can also add a little cottage cheese to the dough. This bread is perfect with coffee.

Total time: 2½ hours | Yield: 1 loaf (2 pounds) / 10 servings
Program: Cake | Crust: Medium

INGREDIENTS

2 whole eggs

¾ cup butter, sliced

1/3 cup whole milk

1 tsp. salt

4 Tbsp. sugar

2¾ cups all-purpose flour, sifted

2 tsp. bread machine yeast

¾ cup raisins

STEPS TO MAKE IT

1. Scald raisins with boiling water, drain, and dry.
2. Place all the dry and liquid ingredients, except raisins, in the pan and follow the instructions for your bread machine.
3. Pay particular attention to measuring the ingredients. Use a measuring cup, measuring spoon, and kitchen scales to do so.
4. Set the baking program to CAKE and the crust type to MEDIUM.
5. Add the raisins after the beep or place them in the dispenser of the bread machine.
6. If the dough is too dense or too wet, adjust the amount of flour and liquid in the recipe.
7. When the program has ended, take the pan out of the bread machine and let cool for 5 minutes.
8. Shake the loaf out of the pan. If necessary, use a spatula.
9. Wrap the bread with a kitchen towel and set it aside for an hour. Otherwise, you can cool it on a wire rack.

NUTRITION GUIDELINES (PER SERVING)

Calories 396; Total Fat 19.1g; Saturated Fat 11.5g; Cholesterol 88; Sodium 436mg; Total Carbohydrate 50.5g; Dietary Fiber 1.9g; Total Sugars 14.7g; Protein 7.1g

APPLE BREAD

This sweet bread with a fluffy crumb is a perfect match for tea. The vanilla flavor fills the air as you are baking the bread and creates a very special mood. The dough won't rise much, but the apple will make this bread fluffy. If your raisins are too dry, soak them in water, apple juice, or brandy in advance.

Total time: 3½ hours | Yield: 1 loaf (2½ pounds) / 12 servings
Program: Basic / White Bread | Crust: Dark

INGREDIENTS

2½ tsp. bread machine yeast

3½ cups bread machine flour, sifted

½ tsp. sea salt

6 Tbsp. sugar

1 bag vanillin

6 Tbsp. extra-virgin olive oil

3 whole eggs

1 cup lukewarm water

1 cup apples, peeled and diced

You can also add nuts or raisins

STEPS TO MAKE IT

1. Place all the dry and liquid ingredients in the pan and follow the instructions for your bread machine.
2. Pay particular attention to measuring the ingredients. Use a measuring cup, measuring spoon, and kitchen scales to do so.
3. Set the baking program to BASIC and the crust type to DARK.
4. If the dough is too dense or too wet, adjust the amount of flour and liquid in the recipe.
5. When the program has ended, take the pan out of the bread machine and let cool for 5 minutes.
6. Shake the loaf out of the pan. If necessary, use a spatula.
7. Wrap the bread with a kitchen towel and set it aside for an hour. Otherwise, you can cool it on a wire rack.

NUTRITION GUIDELINES (PER SERVING)

Calories 379; Total Fat 12.5g; Saturated Fat 1.9g; Cholesterol 61; Sodium 173mg; Total Carbohydrate 59.1g; Dietary Fiber 3.1g; Total Sugars 15.1g; Protein 8.4g

LEMON CAKE

If there's no time to cook a yeast bread, turn to baking powder for a helping hand. Just a couple of hours and your sweet baking is done. Unlike yeast bread, this one can be eaten warm. If you cut it into cubes and bake it in a hot oven, it makes the perfect crunchy snack.

Total time: 2½ hours | Yield: 1 loaf (1½ pounds) / 8 servings
Program: Dough/Bake | Crust: Medium

INGREDIENTS

3 whole eggs
½ cup butter, softened
½ tsp. kosher salt
4/5 cup white sugar
2½ cups whole-grain flour
2½ tsp. baking powder
juice and peel of one small lemon

STEPS TO MAKE IT

1. Combine the eggs, sugar, and salt.
2. Beat with a mixer into a thick foam.
3. Place all the dry and liquid ingredients in the pan and follow the instructions for your bread machine.
4. Pay particular attention to measuring the ingredients. Use a measuring cup, measuring spoon, and kitchen scales to do so.
5. Set the program to DOUGH for 30 minutes.
6. Then bake on the BAKE program for 2 hours.
7. When the program has ended, take the pan out of the bread machine and let cool for 5 minutes.
8. Shake the loaf out of the pan. If necessary, use a spatula.
9. Wrap the bread with a kitchen towel and set it aside for an hour. Otherwise, you can cool it on a wire rack.
10. Sprinkle with powdered sugar.

NUTRITION GUIDELINES (PER SERVING)

Calories 346; Total Fat 13.6g; Saturated Fat 7.9g; Cholesterol 92mg; Sodium 254mg; Total Carbohydrate 51.2g; Dietary Fiber 1.1g; Total Sugars 21g; Protein 6.3g

SOFT COCONUT BREAD

The beautiful dome-shaped top will look even better if, before baking, you carefully brush it with the warm, sweet liquid left after soaking the candied fruit. To keep the top from browning too fast, cover the opening with foil. And if it doesn't quite work out as you hoped, you can always decorate the loaf with some powdered sugar or glazing.

Total time: 3½ hours | Yield: 1 loaf (2 pounds) / 10 servings
Program: Basic | Crust: Medium

INGREDIENTS

¾ cup lukewarm whole milk

2 whole eggs

3 cups bread machine flour, sifted

4 Tbsp. butter, melted

1 tsp. kosher salt

2 Tbsp. white sugar

1 tsp. rum

1 tsp. bread machine yeast

½ cup dried coconut

STEPS TO MAKE IT

1. Place all the dry and liquid ingredients, except the coconut, in the pan and follow the instructions for your bread machine.
2. Pay particular attention to measuring the ingredients. Use a measuring cup, measuring spoon, and kitchen scales to do so.
3. Set the baking program to BASIC and the crust type to MEDIUM.
4. Add the coconut after the beep or place them in the dispenser of the bread machine.
5. If the dough is too dense or too wet, adjust the amount of flour and liquid in the recipe.
6. Before starting the baking process, you can grease the top with a beaten egg and decorate with coconut shavings. Or after baking, cover with syrup and powdered sugar.
7. When the program has ended, take the pan out of the bread machine and let cool for 5 minutes.
8. Shake the loaf out of the pan. If necessary, use a spatula.
9. Wrap the bread with a kitchen towel and set it aside for an hour. Otherwise, you can cool it on a wire rack.

NUTRITION GUIDELINES (PER SERVING)

Calories 367; Total Fat 11.8g; Saturated Fat 7g; Cholesterol 77mg; Sodium 479mg; Total Carbohydrate 54.8g; Dietary Fiber 2.4g; Total Sugars 5.9g; Protein 9.5g

PINEAPPLE COCONUT BREAD

Rather than pineapple, you can use any other kind of candied or exotic fruits.

Total time: 4 hours | Yield: 1 loaf (2½ pounds) / 12 servings
Program: Basic | Crust: Light

INGREDIENTS

2 tsp. bread machine yeast

2 Tbsp. sugar

3¾ cups bread machine flour, sifted

1 tsp. kosher salt

6 Tbsp. coconut shavings

½ cup candied, dried pineapple

1½ Tbsp. rum

1 Tbsp. extra-virgin olive oil

1 cup lukewarm water

STEPS TO MAKE IT

1. Cut pineapple into cubes and douse with boiling water. Do not soak.
2. Place all the dry and liquid ingredients, except the pineapple, in the pan and follow the instructions for your bread machine.
3. Pay particular attention to measuring the ingredients. Use a measuring cup, measuring spoon, and kitchen scales to do so.
4. Set the baking program to BASIC and the crust type to LIGHT.
5. Add the pineapple after the beep or place them in the dispenser of the bread machine.
6. If the dough is too dense or too wet, adjust the amount of flour and liquid in the recipe.
7. When the program has ended, take the pan out of the bread machine and let cool for 5 minutes.
8. Shake the loaf out of the pan. If necessary, use a spatula.
9. Wrap the bread with a kitchen towel and set it aside for an hour. Otherwise, you can cool it on a wire rack.
10. You can sprinkle the hot loaf with powdered sugar.

NUTRITION GUIDELINES (PER SERVING)

Calories 436; Total Fat 7.1g; Saturated Fat 3.4g; Cholesterol 0mg; Sodium 456mg; Total Carbohydrate 81.6g; Dietary Fiber 5.4g; Total Sugars 12.2g; Protein 8.1g

CITRUS BREAD

Choose any juice to your liking to make this bread. Both packaged or freshly squeezed will work equally fine. You can even use juice mixtures, such as multi-fruit, banana, and strawberry, or pear and apple juices. If you want, you can add some water to a smoothie or fruit puree. Soak candied fruit in water, brandy, or juice, and then let it dry on a paper towel and dredge with flour.

Total time: 4 hours | Yield: 1 loaf (2½ pounds) / 12 servings
Program: Basic | Crust: Medium

INGREDIENTS

1 cup orange juice

½ cup lukewarm water

2½ Tbsp. butter, softened

2 Tbsp. powdered milk

2½ Tbsp. brown sugar

1 tsp. kosher salt

4 cups whole-grain flour

1½ tsp. bread machine yeast

¾ cup candied fruits (pineapple, coconut, papaya)

¼ cup walnuts, chopped

1 Tbsp. all-purpose flour for packing candied fruits

¼ cup almond flakes

STEPS TO MAKE IT

1. You can add any juice. The most delicious combinations of juice are multifruit, banana-strawberry, pear-apple
2. Put the candied fruit in water, cognac, or juice; then dry it on a paper towel and roll in flour.
3. Place all the dry and liquid ingredients, except almonds, candied fruits, in the pan, and follow the instructions for your bread machine.
4. Pay particular attention to measuring the ingredients. Use a measuring cup, measuring spoon, and kitchen scales to do so.
5. Set the baking program to BASIC and the crust type to MEDIUM.
6. Add the candied fruits and almond flakes after the beep or place them in the dispenser of the bread machine.
7. If the dough is too dense or too wet, adjust the amount of flour and liquid in the recipe.
8. When the program has ended, take the pan out of the bread machine and let cool for 5 minutes.
9. Shake the loaf out of the pan. If necessary, use a spatula.
10. Wrap the bread with a kitchen towel and set it aside for an hour. Otherwise, you can cool it on a wire rack.

NUTRITION GUIDELINES (PER SERVING)

Calories 313; Total Fat 4.3g; Saturated Fat 2.4g; Cholesterol 10mg; Sodium 331mg; Total Carbohydrate 60.2g; Dietary Fiber 1.9g; Total Sugars 10.6g; Protein 7.8g

ORANGE BREAD

It is delicious to spread orange marmalade on the top and serve with cardamom tea.

Total time: 4 hours | Yield: 1 loaf (2½ pounds) / 12 servings
Program: Basic | Crust: Medium

INGREDIENTS

- 1½ tsp. bread machine yeast
- 3½ cups bread machine flour, sifted
- 1½ tsp. sea salt
- 2 Tbsp. white sugar
- 2 Tbsp. butter, softened
- 1 cup orange juice
- ½ cup milk
- 2 tsp. orange peel
- ½ tsp. ground cardamom
- 1 tsp. turmeric
- dried / fresh cranberries to taste

STEPS TO MAKE IT

1. Place all the dry and liquid ingredients, except berries, in the pan and follow the instructions for your bread machine.
2. Pay particular attention to measuring the ingredients. Use a measuring cup, measuring spoon, and kitchen scales to do so.
3. Set the baking program to BASIC and the crust type to MEDIUM.
4. Add the berries after the beep.
5. If the dough is too dense or too wet, adjust the amount of flour and liquid in the recipe.
6. When the program has ended, take the pan out of the bread machine and let cool for 5 minutes.
7. Shake the loaf out of the pan. If necessary, use a spatula.
8. Wrap the bread with a kitchen towel and set it aside for an hour. Otherwise, you can cool it on a wire rack.

NUTRITION GUIDELINES (PER SERVING)

Calories 261; Total Fat 3.9g; Saturated Fat 2.1g; Cholesterol 9mg; Sodium 467mg; Total Carbohydrate 49.4g; Dietary Fiber 1.9g; Total Sugars 6.5g; Protein 6.7g

STRAWBERRY BREAD

Total time: 4 hours | Yield: 1 loaf (2 pounds) / 10 servings
Program: French Bread | Crust: Medium

INGREDIENTS

1¾ cups lukewarm water

2½ tsp. kosher salt

4 cups bread machine flour, sifted

1 tsp. bread machine yeast

1 cup fresh strawberries, chopped

STEPS TO MAKE IT

1. Place all the dry and liquid ingredients, except strawberries, in the pan and follow the instructions for your bread machine.
2. Pay particular attention to measuring the ingredients. Use a measuring cup, measuring spoon, and kitchen scales to do so.
3. Set the baking program to FRENCH BREAD and the crust type to MEDIUM.
4. Add the strawberries after the beep.
5. If the dough is too dense or too wet, adjust the amount of flour and liquid in the recipe.
6. When the program has ended, take the pan out of the bread machine and let cool for 5 minutes.
7. Shake the loaf out of the pan. If necessary, use a spatula.
8. Wrap the bread with a kitchen towel and set it aside for an hour. Otherwise, you can cool it on a wire rack.

NUTRITION GUIDELINES (PER SERVING)

Calories 313; Total Fat 0.9g; Saturated Fat 0.1g; Cholesterol 0mg; Sodium 973g; Total Carbohydrate 65.7g; Dietary Fiber 2.9g; Total Sugars 1.4 g; Protein 9g

PEACH BREAD

Whole-grain bread is always dense and heavy. If you want to make bread that is lighter and fluffier, add some finely ground wheat flour. But do not forget to adjust the dough's consistency to make it smooth and not sticky. This bread tastes especially good with butter or jam.

Total time: 4 hours | Yield: 1 loaf (2 pounds) / 10 servings
Program: Whole-Grain Bread | Crust: Medium

INGREDIENTS

4 cups wholemeal flour

2 tsp. bread machine yeast

1¼ cups lukewarm water

1½ Tbsp. flaxseed oil

1½ Tbsp. brown sugar

1 ½ tsp. kosher salt

2 peaches, peeled and diced

STEPS TO MAKE IT

1. Place all the dry and liquid ingredients, except peaches, in the pan and follow the instructions for your bread machine.
2. Pay particular attention to measuring the ingredients. Use a measuring cup, measuring spoon, and kitchen scales to do so.
3. Set the baking program to WHOLE-GRAIN BREAD and the crust type to MEDIUM.
4. Add the peaches after the beep.
5. If the dough is too dense or too wet, adjust the amount of flour and liquid in the recipe.
6. When the program has ended, take the pan out of the bread machine and let cool for 5 minutes.
7. Shake the loaf out of the pan. If necessary, use a spatula.
8. Wrap the bread with a kitchen towel and set it aside for an hour. Otherwise, you can cool it on a wire rack.

NUTRITION GUIDELINES (PER SERVING)

Calories 246; Total Fat 4g; Saturated Fat 0.3g; Cholesterol 0mg; Sodium 440g; Total Carbohydrate 44.3g; Dietary Fiber 6.4g; Total Sugars 5.8 g; Protein 8.2g

Useful Tools

MEASURING CUP

All the dry ingredients are measured with a measuring cup and a measuring spoon. They usually come with the bread machine.

KITCHEN SCALES

If you need a more exact measurement of dry ingredients, use kitchen scales. Along with that, you should always consider the percentage of moisture in specific ingredients and take it into account to get the desired consistency.

MIXER

To get a stronger dough, you should first pre-mix some of the ingredients with a mixer.

WIRE WHISK

Sometimes it is enough to manually whisk the ingredients.

PLASTIC SPATULA

Sometimes it is not that easy to get the bread out of the pan. Use the spatula to manage it quickly and easily.

SHARP KNIFE

You'll need a sharp to make fine cuts on the dough.

SIEVE

The final product will be finer and softer if you sift the flour before adding it to the pan.

BRUSH

In some recipes, you'll need to brush the dough with milk, butter, or a beaten egg to get a gorgeous crust at the end.

KITCHEN TIMER

Of course, the bread machine is equipped with a timer, but isn't it convenient to know which mode is on at the moment?

METAL RACK

This is exactly what you need to properly cool your fresh-baked loaf. Just take the bread out of the bread machine and leave it on the wire rack for an hour. It will cool evenly on all sides.

FROM THE AUTHOR

Until I got my **own bread machine**, I knew nothing about bread except for the fact that it was bought in a shop. Then I discovered that **making bread at home was easy and fun**. I wanted to learn more about it and to try something new, to improve my skills, and to make my tasty homemade bread even tastier.

The internet is full of all the information a person might need, but surfing for the right pieces of it takes a lot of time and effort. Looking for answers to my amateurish questions made me read through countless complex professional texts.

How much did I wish I'd had a book with simple step-by-step explanations?

Perhaps, that is the main reason why I've written this one.

Now, as I am writing these words, **the bread machine is on, filling my apartment with the fragrance of freshly baked bread**. There is nothing like it. Bread is bread. And **where the bread is, there is a home**. The bread machine takes on all the grunt work, and bread making becomes really simple. Simple — but not boring!

I hope this book will let you enjoy bread making in your home!

OUR RECOMMENDATIONS

Dutch Oven Cookbook: Great Recipes for Dutch Oven Cooking in Just One Pot

Sous Vide Cookbook: Delicious Foolproof Sous Vide Recipes for Perfect, No-Fuss Meals at Home

I'd like to express my gratitude and heartfelt appreciation to everyone I've learned from! Without your books and articles, and the exchange of experience with my fellow bakers, I'd never know all that I know about bread today, and I wouldn't have this opportunity to share my knowledge with others.

If you enjoy the book or find it useful, leave your review of the book, please. Your feedback is essential for other readers and for us to make the right choice.

If you have any questions, feel free to contact me

www.goodreads.com/author/show/8342253.Linda_Gilmore

www.facebook.com/linda.gilmore28

Recipe Index

A

APPLE BREAD 82

B

Carrot Oat Bread 66

Celery Bread 76

Cheddar Sausage Bread 56

Cheese Bread 28

Chicken Bread 50

Citrus Bread 78

Citrus Bread 90

Classic White Bread 10

Coconut Bran Bread 12

Coffee Rye Bread 26

Corn Bread 20

CORN BREAD 8

Cream Hazelnut Bread 22

Crispy Bread with Fried Onion 60

Cumin Bread 36

Cumin Tomato Bread 70

CURD BREAD 58

E

Everyday Bread 8

F

Fragrant Cinnamon Bread 46

French Ham Bread 48

From the Author 99

G

Green Cheese Bread 30

H

Herb Bread 32

L

Lemon Cake 84

M

Meat Bread 48

Milk White Bread 14

Mozzarella Bread 44

Mozzarella Whole-Grain Bread 40

O

Olive Bread 34

ONION BACON BREAD 52

Orange Bread 92

Our Recommendations 100

P

PEACH BREAD 96

Pineapple Coconut Bread 88

Poppy Seeds Bread 24

R

Raisin Bread 38

RAISIN CAKE 80

Rosemary Bread 42

S

Saffron Tomato Bread 64

Savory Horseradish Bread 72

Savory Tomato Cheese Bread 62

Soft Coconut Bread 86

Sour Cream Wheat Bread 16

Spice Bread 28

STRAWBERRY BREAD 94

Sweet Bread 78

U

Useful Tools 98

V

Vanilla Milk Bread 18

VEGETABLE BREAD 54

Vegetable Bread 58

Vegetable Bread 74

Z

Zucchini Bread 68

Copyright

ALL ©COPYRIGHTS RESERVED 2019 by Linda Gilmore

All Rights Reserved. No part of this publication or the information in it may be quoted from or reproduced in any form by means such as printing, scanning, photocopying, or otherwise without prior written permission of the copyright holder.

Disclaimer and Terms of Use: Effort has been made to ensure that the information in this book is accurate and complete; however, the author and the publisher do not warrant the accuracy of the information, text, or graphics contained within the book due to the rapidly changing nature of science, research, known and unknown facts, and the internet. The author and the publisher do not hold any responsibility for errors, omissions, or contrary interpretation of the subject matter herein. This book is presented solely for motivational and informational purposes only.

Made in the USA
San Bernardino, CA
14 March 2020